THE LIFE & TIMES OF

Pablo Picasso

BY
Esme Hawes

SIENA

This is a Siena book
Siena is an imprint of Parragon Book Service Ltd

This edition first published by
Parragon Book Service Ltd in 1996

Parragon Book Service Ltd
Unit 13–17 Avonbridge Trading Estate
Atlantic Road, Avonmouth
Bristol BS11 9QD

Produced by Magpie Books Ltd, London

Copyright © Parragon Book Service Ltd 1996

Illustrations courtesy of: Bridgeman Art Library; Hulton
Deutsch Collection; London Features International; Peter
Newark's Historical Pictures; Popperfoto.

Works by Picasso © Succession Picasso/D.A.C.S. 1996

ISBN 0 75251 551 9

A copy of the British Library Cataloguing in Publication
Data is available from the British Library.

Typeset by Whitelaw & Palmer Ltd, Glasgow

MÁLAGA

On 25 October 1881, Doña María Picasso, the wife of Don José Ruiz, a painter and part-time art teacher, gave birth to their first child, a much-longed for son and heir to the Ruiz family name. They lived in Málaga, an ancient city in the far south of Spain. Though Málaga was, at that time, the country's second most important sea port, it was still a simple place of 120,000 inhabitants, twenty-seven churches and four monasteries. No tourists arrived and no locals left.

It was a city steeped in history, settled in in turn by Phoenicians, Romans, Visigoths and then, for 776 years, the Moors, who left an indelible Islamic mark behind them. To the sophisticated people of Madrid or Barcelona, the Andalucia region in the south was, therefore, a foreign place, filled with barbarians, harsh-sounding dialects and insurgent peoples, constantly rebelling against their alien rulers. In 1831, fifty revolutionaries had been shot in the very square in which Picasso was born – a pattern of rebellion set to be repeated throughout the nineteenth century.

Despite this tumultuous atmosphere, Málaga remained all the while a profoundly Catholic place and, just sixteen days after his birth, Pablo Ruiz Picasso (for in Spain a child takes both his mother's and father's surnames) was taken to the parish church of Santiago el Mayor, where he was duly christened 'Pablo, Diego, José, Francisco de Paul, Juan Nepomuceno, María de los Remedios, Cipriano de la Santísima Trinidad'. And, as if this wasn't enough of an ordeal, he was also covered with a sprinkling of salt in order to thrust out the Devil.

This plethora of first names by no means implied that the family was noble. Picasso's paternal grandfather, Diego Ruiz, was, in fact, a glovemaker during age in which there was little call for gloves. He married a local beauty, one María de la Paz Blasco y Echevarria, and the couple had eleven children, one of whom was José, Picasso's father. As a young man José had high hopes of his talent as an illustrator and he insisted, despite his family's dismay, that he was destined to become a professional artist. Eking out a meagre living by producing pictures of lilacs and pigeons, he lived with his eldest brother, a canon, who also supported two unmarried sisters.

In 1868 the local theatre needed redecorating and two quite well known Valencian artists arrived to do the work. These two fellows stayed on for a while after they had finished and gave a few lessons at the local art school, as well as setting up a small museum of fine arts on the second floor of a former monastery. José leapt at the chance to become the museum's curator and, for some years, revelled in his new-found contentment. His parents, however, were getting impatient. They urged him to marry. He was almost forty years old and not one of their eleven children had yet produced a son. María

Pablo Picasso

Picasso y Lopez, a suitable spinster, was found but José wasn't immediately enthusiastic about the match. He held out for his liberty for some years until, eventually, he could no longer take the pressure and the couple married in 1880. Although his new wife's unique surname was said to display Catalan, Moorish or Jewish roots, no one ever really knew its true origin. The very year after the wedding, however, María came up with the goods and the new baby was called Pablo Ruiz Picasso.

By 1887 the couple also had two daughters but José was still more interested in his job at the museum. The municipality cut his salary by half and, in order to survive, José was forced to give private painting lessons. He was becoming increasingly disillusioned with his family and with life. Pablo, on the other hand, was having a whale of a time. The only boy in a generation of daughters, he spent his entire childhood being spoilt and pampered by women. The only times at which he saw his distant and spiritually crushed father were on the rare occasion when José took his son to one of the exclusively masculine bullfights that they both so adored.

After suffering a minor kidney infection, Pablo was labelled a 'delicate' child and immediately sent to a private school. His spelling was highly idiosyncratic and he was slow at both reading and mathematics. Though never actually naughty, he spent most of his time staring out of the schoolroom window and then attempting to replicate everything he saw in crayon, all over his textbooks.

Don José didn't care. He taught his son to wash paintbrushes and to stretch canvas. Pablo loved every second of it. The ten-year-old would draw the colour and ritual of the bullring over and over again, and life was very pleasant for him until the municipality decided to close the museum altogether. It was a disaster.

Eventually, Don José found a new teaching post at La Coruña, a port in north-west Spain. A family friend gave Pablo, who was still virtually unable to read or write, an elementary school certificate and the family set off for La Coruña in 1891. It was the first time that the boy had ever been to sea.

La Coruña was rainy and cold. Gone was the idyllic life of Andalucia and the sunny world in which Pablo had been understood. The locals of La Coruña spoke not Spanish, but Gallego, and the only interesting thing in the whole town was a Roman tower. He sketched the rainswept harbour, the pigeons and the local people, and José, a broken man, taught his son the techniques of pen and ink, charcoal and pastel. He was a rigorous disciplinarian, but his son's talents shone through almost immediately. By 1894 he was able to produce a perfectly proportioned oil of a bald man with a beard. He was thirteen. By 1895 he was already outshining his father. José acknowledged his son's superiority and solemnly handed over his brushes to Pablo, never to paint again. In disgust at his father's apparent weakness, the boy began to sign his name 'P. Picasso', after his mother, rather than the full 'P. Ruiz Picasso'. After 1901, he never used Ruiz again.

Times were hard for José and, to add to his woes, in1895 his youngest daughter fell ill and died. When one of his former assistants, who now worked in a famous art school in Barcelona, suggested a job-swap, José jumped at the opportunity. The new post would mean an escape from the old, damp house, a higher salary and a Mediterranean climate once more. The Ruiz family set off for the north-east.

BARCELONA

In 1895 Barcelona was a prestigious European city with over half a million inhabitants, almost all of whom spoke Catalán. During the Middle Ages Catalonia had been an independent country, held for a while by both the Moors and Charlemagne, only to be declared independent by Wilfred the Shaggy. It became a proud trading nation with splendid literature, architecture and universities. After much fighting, however, Barcelona was eventually conquered by the Castilians, who ruled the rest of Spain. The Catalán language was suppressed whilst the university was closed down. By 1895 some of this repression had been lifted but the city was still ruled by fervent nationalist and separatist emotions. Its people felt that they were part of a civilised culture, crushed by a centralised and vulgar one. Anarchy was preached all over the city.

Don José chose a dark house, a hundred yards from the art school, in the centre of the old city. The school itself was situated in an eighteenth-century building by the harbour and Don José immediately determined that his son should be taken on as a star pupil. Though his colleagues were quite prepared to believe that his thirteen-year-old son could draw quite well, the average first-year students were twenty years old, and the teachers therefore insisted that Pablo submit himself to some

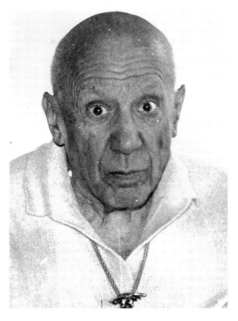

Picasso

very rigorous testing. He had twenty-four hours to complete two set tasks: drawings of a model draped in a sheet and a standing nude. In less than an hour he had finished both. He was immediately admitted to the higher of the two entrance streams, along with 127 other men.

In his very first anatomy class, Picasso sat next to a powerful youth called Manuel Pallarès Grau. The pair became firm friends, despite the obvious difference in age. Pablo, in fact, was immediately accepted by the whole school by virtue of his outstanding talent and his charming personality. When not at school, he spent his time roaming the streets with Pallarès, who took him to a brothel. As soon as he had been fully initiated in anatomy, Picasso also began to draw the female form.

Don José, who had channelled all of his frustrated artistic ambitions into his son, hired Pablo a studio in which to paint. It was a tiny, ill-lit room, just around the corner from the family home, but it brought Picasso independence and he worked hard there. The first result was a large oil called *Science and Charity* which, though conservative and traditional, was loved by his family. Proudly, they sent it to the National Exhibition in Madrid, where it received an 'honourable mention'; they then sent it to the Provincial Competition in Málaga where, not unnaturally, it won the gold medal. It was a perfectly accomplished work, but it was also Picasso's farewell to the academic tradition of printing. His rich uncle Salvador, however, unaware of this development, offered to pay for Picasso to go to Madrid and study at the Academy of San Fernando.

It was the autumn of 1897, and Picasso took the pitiful sum of money that his uncle had offered him and found himself, on his sixteenth birthday, in a cheap hotel in Madrid, entirely alone. Once again he passed an entrance exam with stupefying ease, only to find that the teaching in Madrid was almost as uninspiring as that of Barcelona. Instead of attending lectures, he went to the great Prado Museum, where he copied works by the great Spanish masters: Goya, Velázquez and El Greco. Uncle Salvador heard that his nephew was skipping classes and immediately cut off his allowance. Picasso could barely afford to eat. He fell ill with a violent fever. Life in Madrid was unbearable and, as soon as he was able, he went back to Barcelona. His old friend Pallarès took him home to the deepest Catalonian countryside and Picasso enjoyed it so much that the two of them stayed for nine months. By the time they returned, in 1898, he could speak fluent Catalán, and this gave him an entrée to Barcelona's artistic society.

It was a society modelled on Parisian lines. A group of men, united in their love of modernism, met regularly at a café called 'Els Quatre Gats', where they discussed anything and everything heatedly in Catalán. The café was the epicentre of the Barcelona avant-garde, and in a room at the back, there were puppet shows and exhibitions. Picasso, now seventeen, wanted to be in the thick of it all. He left home and went to live in a brothel, where he paid his way by decorating the walls with elaborate murals. After a short while, however, he began sharing a flat with one of his trendy new friends, Carlos Casagemas –

through whom he met Jaime Sabartès who went on to become his lifelong secretary and biographer.

Although Picasso still had very little formal education, and though he could still barely read, he was now surrounded by people who had and could. Through them he learnt about writers like Ibsen and Nietzsche, and about all of the modern things that were happening in that great city, Paris. They encouraged Picasso to paint, and in February 1900 he gave a little exhibition of portrait drawings – though his technique was improving, he was still only a talented student at this time. He was, however, becoming increasingly keen to go to Paris, the only place where, realistically, he could now develop as an artist, and, in the autumn of 1900, Picasso and Casagemas set off northwards to find modern art.

Pallarès arrived in the French capital just two days after his two friends, to find the pair already ensconced in a small studio in Montmartre with a girlfriend apiece. During the day Picasso went to the Louvre and looked at the Impressionists, learning about contemporary artists like Seurat, Redon and Toulouse-Lautrec. During the nights he painted. Wandering the streets, he saw for the first time the paintings of Cézanne, Degas and Gauguin, all on sale in private galleries for a few francs each. For Picasso, it was heaven.

Through contacts from home, Picasso came across a small-time dealer called Pedro Manyac, who saw his paintings and was impressed. He offered to pay the young artist a salary of 150 francs a month, for which he would retain all of Picasso's output. Picasso, still only nineteen, had never seen so much money at one time. Of course he said 'yes'.

On the home front, Casagemas's girlfriend had abandoned him for one of the other young talents of the group. Casagemas became depressed, and began drinking heavily. Picasso took his friend home for Christmas but nothing seemed to help. The pair went on to Málaga, but the Ruiz family were still angry with young Picasso for wasting their money in Madrid and they turned him away. Picasso was profoundly upset by this rejection and never again set foot in Málaga – instead he returned to Barcelona. Casagemas was also upset. He returned to Paris, where he invited his old girlfriend and her new lover to dinner. Smiling as they all sat down for soup, he took out a gun and shot himself in the head.

In June 1901, Picasso finally returned to Paris, only to discover that Manyac had already arranged an exhibition of his work at a highly prestigious gallery. This show opened on 24 June 1901 and contained seventy-five paintings, mostly of bullfights and café nightlife. Critics turned up and he was favourably reviewed, though it was only Manyac, the agent, who actually profited if any of the pictures were sold. One critic, in particular, admired Picasso's work and sought out his acquaintance – this was Max Jacob, a poet and writer. He called on Picasso at Manyac's flat, only to find him sitting on the bare floor surrounded by a swarm of poor Spanish painters, all eating and talking at the same time. Jacob could speak no Spanish, Picasso no French, yet the two men instantly became firm friends, while Picasso and Manyac rapidly fell out.

Picasso began to produce work about the suicide of his friend Casagemas. Over and over, he returned to the morbid subject, and each of the paintings, sometimes two or three a day, were suffused with the mournful colour blue. This marked the onset of what was to become known as his 'Blue Period'. The most significant picture he did at this time is called *The Burial of Casagemas*, and shows a group of mourners gathered at a funeral. Three naked prostitutes look upwards at the clouds and a white horse carries a dark-clothed man into the clouds. Art historians have debated at length about this picture. El Greco, Odilon Redon and Paul Cézanne have all been cited as influences. Picasso himself was never a man of words and he rarely gave his pictures titles (most of these were added later by critics). Manyac, in particular, was distressed by his client's

La Vie, 1903 by Picasso

morbid turn of mood and begged Picasso to abandon blue, not knowing that, in later years, these paintings would achieve some of the highest prices ever paid for the work of a living painter.

Not long afterwards, Picasso painted a half-length self-portrait in which he appears, bearded, muffled in a dark greatcoat with a high collar. It was a masterpiece, highly reminiscent of a well-known painting by Vincent van Gogh but, just like the work of the man who had inspired it, no one would buy it. Picasso, whose relationship with Manyac had now soured beyond endurance, wrote home begging for the fare to return to Barcelona.

Back in Spain, he continued to work primarily in blue – the two most successful paintings of the period being of a child holding a dove and of a little girl eating soup. He also began to sculpt. Manyac, meanwhile, held on to some of Picasso's work and, though the contract between them was terminated, arranged another exhibition at which he sold one painting for 250 francs and a second for 150. Picasso, however, didn't receive even enough money for a ticket back to Paris – he had to wait until October 1902 before he had enough for the fare. On his return, he encountered Max Jacob, who invited him to share his studio. Jacob was working as a shop assistant in the daytime and slept at night; Picasso painted at night and slept during the day – a convenient arrangement which meant that they could both live in one tiny studio, taking turns with the bed. By the end of the year, however, even this temporary haven was proving too expensive. Picasso hadn't sold a single picture and neither man had money for food or heating. They shivered and they starved. By January 1903 Picasso was reduced to burning his drawings for firewood. It was the hardest time he had ever known and he came close to giving up in despair. Yet, just a few days later, having reached a point at which he was ready to give up art for ever, someone bought one of his paintings – *Maternity* – for over 200 francs. Picasso took the money and returned to Barcelona.

He now started work on a large painting, *La Vie*. In many ways this was to be his final statement on the suicide of his friend Casagemas, who appears in the picture, gaunt and ghostly, pointing at a woman, reminiscent of the Virgin Mary, who clutches a sickly-looking child. It is a spectral, deathly work, and proved to be a kind of exorcism for the artist, since it was to be one of the very last of the blue paintings.

In May 1904 Picasso set off once more for Paris, this time for good. He rented an unfurnished studio, stole Max Jacob's only pair of trousers, and started an affair with a placid, dopey woman called Fernande Olivier, the wife of an insane sculptor from whom she was separated. Guillaume Apollinaire, the not-yet-famous French poet, helped Picasso make his flat look just a little more inviting for Fernande's first visit. He obviously did a good job since, soon afterwards, she moved in for good. Picasso was inordinately proud and insanely jealous of his large, indolent girlfriend, and hated it when she went out without him. It was fortunate, therefore, that she was the kind of woman who didn't like to move anywhere unless there was a very good reason. Mostly she stayed indoors, lying around or entertaining a group of Picasso's friends, who now included the painters Georges Braque and André Derain, and the playwright Alfred Jarry. The whole group began to go to the local circus three or four times a week, where Picasso drew the acrobats, the tumblers and the clowns.

He built these sketches up into a work called *Les Saltimbanques*, a very large picture featuring a harlequin, an elderly jester and a small girl. This has been called 'the last painting of the nineteenth century', and it is certainly an atmospheric work. It has red and orange in it, as well as blue and white, and it possesses a poised, statuesque quality. In style, it replies to the French classical tradition and it seems to convey the idea that there can be a relationship between the academic and the avant-garde styles. At the time, this was a highly revolutionary idea.

FIRST SUCCESS

In November 1905, Gertrude Stein and her brother Leo, eminent American writers, wandered into a Paris art gallery where they caught sight of a few paintings they admired, and which they bought on the spot. One of them was by Picasso. Leo was more enthusiastic than Gertrude, who did not like *Fillette à la Corbeille Fleurie* since she found the child's big feet and legs repulsive. Still, Leo was keen and the gallery owner took the couple to meet the artist, whom they liked, immediately buying 800 francs' worth of his pictures. They invited Picasso and Fernande to dinner and, though none of the parties involved could speak the other's language, Picasso asked Gertrude Stein to sit for him, which she did some eighty or ninety times. Most important, the Steins knew a large number of other rich Americans all of whom came to their house and saw the fashionable new artist's work displayed on the walls. They also introduced Picasso to the influential Fauvist painter Henri Matisse.

Picasso was still only twenty-four. Matisse was thirty-five and, though desperately poor, the leader of the Fauve movement, as well as being an outstanding and controversial figure in the art world. He was also married, with a small daughter, and, though the two men were unlike in every way, he became the one artist to whose work Picasso referred throughout his life. He also did Picasso the great favour of introducing him to a Russian millionaire called Sergei Ichukhin, who also bought two of his paintings. Picasso was almost overwhelmed with riches, and began to paint all in pink.

Towards the end of 1906 he completed a portrait of Gertrude Stein, which she loved. In it, her features are depicted as having the character of an immobile, severe mask, and the whole image has a strange, surreal quality. The Steins were impressed, and encouraged Picasso to begin work on a series of drawings for a great canvas. Originally this was to depict a brothel with a sailor figure at the centre but, by the time he finished, in 1907, it had become an almost decontextualised picture of five prostitutes with all trace of feeling removed. The pink heads are sharply angled, the pink bodies are made of straight, disjointed lines. The features of the squatting figure (the four others are standing) are savagely, almost painfully, jumbled. Picasso had, to all intents and purposes, effectively invented Cubism and his friends, on being invited to view the work, stood stunned. They were unable to comprehend this harsh and apparently emotionless view of the world, but what they were looking at was *Les Demoiselles d'Avignon* (as it became known) – one of the most important paintings of the twentieth century.

RECOGNITION

Picasso's agent, seeing *Les Demoiselles d'Avignon*, thought he'd gone mad. Though the painter himself had no doubts about the importance of the work, he rolled the canvas away and ignored it for ten years. In 1904 he had moved into a building called the Bateau-Lavoir ('laundry barge'), and now he concentrated on having a good time. In the autumn of 1908 he decided to give a banquet in honour of his ancient friend, the painter Henri Rousseau, known as 'Le Douanier'.

The guest list was a roll-call of the fashionable artistic world. Gertrude and Leo Stein came, Alice B. Toklas, Gertrude's companion and lover, turned up, and the painter Georges Braque brought Apollinaire. Two of the guests got into a fight and one had to be locked into a cupboard. A third ate Alice Toklas's new hat and a box of matches. Rousseau himself slept through much of the feast, and at three in the morning the Steins took him home. The sixty-four-year-old said it was the best evening of his life.

Picasso was by this time one of the senior residents at the Bateau-Lavoir, which had become something of an artists' commune. Max Jacob also lived there now, as did Amedeo Modigliani, Kees van Dongen, a leading Fauvist, and Juan Gris, recently arrived from Madrid. Picasso spent hours alone with Braque and, by that autumn, they had discovered that their work had developed along much the same lines. Braque submitted his painting to the Salon of 1908, but Matisse, the chairman, was shocked by its linear quality and rejected most of what he called the 'little cubes'. An agent, Daniel-Heni Kahnweiler, who also owned a gallery, liked the paintings, however, and a leading critic, Louis Vauxcelles, wrote a review praising them and the artist's courage. 'He despises form and reduces everything to geometrical diagrams, to cubes,' he said, and the name stuck. By 1909 Picasso and Braque, together with Fernand Léger, Francis Picabia, Gris and Robert Delaunay, had collectively become known as the Cubists.

SIGNS OF FAME

Picasso had always hated poverty and by 1909 he was able to move out of the Bateau-Lavoir and into a relatively sumptuous flat in the Boulevard de Clichy. He and Fernande would sleep until eleven each morning, and they had a live-in maid. Normally the artist ate little and drank only mineral water, but he was starting to appreciate the finer things in life and he began to buy antique furniture and to give sophisticated dinner-parties. His was now a very different world from that of the starving artist, and it was populated by very different people. The old, casual crowd fell away and the most frequent visitor was Braque, who came to talk about their work, which became more and more abstracted, and was largely misunderstood. One nude study, when taken to America, was thought to be a painting of a fire-escape.

One evening, in autumn 1911, Apollinaire turned up out of the blue, looking desperate. Leonardo's *Mona Lisa* had been stolen from the Louvre, and everyone knew that two statues, which Apollinaire had been given as a present many years earlier, had also been stolen from the museum. Though he had nothing to do with the thefts, Apollinaire was a natural suspect and he was arrested and sent to jail, albeit briefly, for possession of the statues. Picasso, who was still very much the foreigner and always suspicious of the French police, was convinced that he too was being followed. He developed a fear of the law that was to stay with him for life, and he grew increasingly depressed until, quite out of the blue, he met Marcelle Humbert, whom he called Éva. Within a few days, the couple had run away to Avignon, where they rented a house. Braque arrived with his new wife and rented the house next door.

It was a time of renewed energy for both men. Their work became less formal and they used softer colours, as well as collage techniques. Kahnweiler, the agent, sold more of his increasingly well-known client's work, and he found Picasso a new flat in Paris. His paintings were exhibited in London, Munich, Cologne and Moscow, and Kahnweiler became Picasso's exclusive agent. More of

Picasso's work was sent to New York for the Armory exhibition, which introduced Cubism to the United States, but Éva fell ill in America. The pair returned to Paris and, by 1914, curves had returned to his work. Dots appeared, and bright slashes of colour. *Les Saltimbanques* was resold for 11,500 francs and, though Picasso did not receive the money, it was still a momentous event. What looked like being a happy and golden age for Picasso was rudely shattered by the outside world. The year was 1914, and it brought war.

WAR YEARS

At the outbreak of the First World War, almost all of Picasso's friends went into the services. Picasso himself, being Spanish, was exempted from war service, but his output decreased, while Kahnweiler, a German, had all his goods confiscated and fled to neutral Switzerland. Leo and Gertrude Stein fell out and their art collection was split in two. Juan Gris, who had no passport, was in hiding, and, to top it all, in the winter of 1915, Éva died of tuberculosis. Seven people attended her funeral.

With Jean Cocteau at a bullfight

Picasso, desperately unhappy, moved into a small, suburban house on the outskirts of Paris. In 1916 he once more met up with the composer, Erik Satie, whom he had known earlier; when the poet Jean Cocteau, at that time twenty-seven, came back on leave later that year he suggested that the three men collaborate on a ballet. Picasso had never been to a ballet, but it was a new project, something that might take his mind off his troubles. In February 1917 he and Cocteau set off for Rome there to meet Sergei Diaghilev, the famous leader of the Ballets Russes, which was to stage and perform the new ballet. One of the dancers was a striking-looking Russian called Olga Koklova, whose command of the French language was even poorer than Picasso's. He immediately took up with her.

Assisted by a huge team of workers, he began

sketching for the sets in Rome, and the eventual result – *Parade* – opened in Paris on 17 May. The plot featured a woman dressed in cowboy boots and a top hat and some acrobats who turned up and did a bit of boxing. It was surrealist before anyone knew what that meant – indeed, Apollinaire coined the term to describe this ballet. The critics hated it, one of them describing it as absolute rubbish. Satie, who had composed the music, wrote this man a rude postcard and was sent to prison for a week for defamation. This was perhaps the only constructive outcome of the whole event.

On 12 July 1918 Picasso and Olga were married in the Russian church on the rue Daru with all due Orthodox pomp and ceremony, and the couple went on honeymoon to Biarritz. He had now found a new agent and a new flat, a fine flat on the sixth floor of a building just off the Champs-Élysées. In November Picasso heard that his old friend, Apollinaire, by then thirty-nine and wounded in the war, had died from the Spanish 'flu on the very day the Armistice was declared. Deeply moved by this evidence of mortality, it was many years before Picasso could paint another self-portrait. His old world was gone. Fernande was absent; Apollinaire dead; Braque had been seriously wounded, which changed both his health and his temper; Derain, too, had been severely affected by the war. It was time to take a new approach to painting, one possessed of a revolutionary and colossal style.

Meanwhile, *Parade* was taken to London, opening there in summer 1919. Picasso, as the set and costume designer, and his wife lived it up like royalty, staying at the Savoy and going on frenzied shopping expeditions. They were wined and dined by the Bloomsbury set and returned to France just in time to catch some sunbathing on the Côte d'Azur. Picasso became one of Paris' top socialites, eating out continually and dressing Olga in little Chanel numbers. He no longer saw his old friends who, in any event, thought that he had sold out. He drew portraits of all his new best friends (some of whom he hadn't actually met), including the composer Igor Stravinsky and the painter Auguste Renoir.

CLASSICISM

Influenced by his stay in the Mediterranean with its Graeco-Roman heritage, Picasso began painting mythological creatures – centaurs, fauns, figures of Pan. Times were calm and smooth, and in February 1921 Olga gave birth to a son, Paulo. His father, ever the Spaniard, was thrilled, and immediately began one of the many, many sketches of childhood and maternity that were soon to flow forth. He also began two versions of a picture which is generally considered to be both the high-water mark of Cubism, and Picasso's farewell to it. Both canvasses are called *Three Musicians with Masks*, and depict huge figures with tiny hands. While both of these paintings looked backwards, Picasso also completed *Three Women at the Fountain*, a painting which shows signs of the neo-classical period that was to come. The canvas is massive and the women in it, and particularly their hands, are huge. They sit on the white rocks with their sausage fingers, motionless and passive.

Picasso designed the set for a new work by Cocteau – an adaptation of Sophocles's *Antigone* – and he continued to live the high life, attending one banquet in honour of Stravinsky at which Marcel Proust and James Joyce were also guests. For Picasso, the company of these three world-renowned men was a far cry from the old days at the Bateau-

Lavoir. He was beginning to lose touch with mere mortals, and began dressing like a dandy, often wearing a traditional Catalan *faixa* (coloured silk waistband). Over and over he painted his son, most famously dressed up as a harlequin, and Olga began playing the prima donna, hiring a nursemaid to hold Paulo's hand and walk with him three paces behind the couple.

Picasso became unhappy with his lot, however. In 1925 he produced a violent, convulsive picture, *La Danse*, which shows huge, barbaric figures of women, looking savage. The left-hand female figure has a saw-edged ribcage, a mad-looking head, fingers reminiscent of claws. It is a terrible picture of destructive womanhood, and one which was to be redrawn constantly throughout Picasso's life.

Olga, too, was discontented. Picasso was undoubtedly a difficult husband, prone to mood swings and violent rages, and she didn't even like his paintings. Both grew gloomy. Olga, once a lithe young ballerina, was now a plump mother. Picasso began painting her as fat and then as a grotesque caricature. He had stopped painting his son altogether. *Woman in an Armchair*, painted in January 1927, shows a distorted figure with a snout-like face and a snoring mouth. The body is amoeba-like, and a lethal trap. Life no longer seemed fair to Picasso. While his male friends died all around him, his wife continued to live. Picasso began a series of beach pictures all of which featured women, sometimes fitting keys into locks, their sexual organs distended and menacing. These pictures culminated in *Bather Seated Beside the Sea* in which the figure of the woman is smooth, and seems to have no trunk at all. She is a praying mantis figure – swallower and devourer of men. Picasso was now the best-known painter in Europe and yet he looked back longingly to the simple days in the Bateau-Lavoir. There was, however, a new reason for his dissatisfaction.

MARIE-THÉRÈSE

In January 1927, Picasso went shopping at the
Galeries Lafayette in Paris, and there met a
young woman called Marie-Thérèse Walter,
who was not yet eighteen years old. Picasso
was fifty. She was beautiful, affectionate,
undemanding, and had never heard of him –
she was also the only one of Picasso's women
never to make money out of the relationship
in later years by writing a book. Picasso
immediately fell for her, and after six months
of her resistance, took her to bed. He felt like

a new man, and began painting some of his most famous pictures, showing Marie-Thérèse in all her serenity and simplicity. He didn't, however, tell Olga.

The first major Picasso retrospective opened on 15 June 1932, and was the highlight of the Paris season. The Hungarian photographer Brassaï involved him in a new magazine called *Minotaure*, which first came out in June 1933 and one of whose illustrators was Salvador Dalí, then twenty-two. Picasso supported Dalí and his glamorous girlfriend, who had until recently been the wife of the poet, and Picasso's friend, Paul Éluard and he lent Dalí the money to go to America. He also did a series of classical etchings of Marie-Thérèse, naked in the lap of a friendly minotaur, and began a painting called *Murder* in which a hideous old hag, closely resembling Olga, stabs a fainting and beautiful Marie-Thérèse figure.

In early 1935 Picasso asked Olga for a divorce. The position was highly complicated since divorce was still illegal in Spain and, in any event, Olga was bitterly opposed to such a step. Eventually, in July 1935, she left, retaining the château Picasso had bought in 1930 and custody of Paulo, while he got the Paris flat and all the paintings. But a child, it seemed, was not irreplaceable, and he now had a new one to play with – a daughter by Marie-Thérèse called Maïa. His old friend from Barcelona, Jaime Sabartès, returned from South America and, while his wife became the housekeeper, Sabartès himself became a constant companion. Picasso stopped painting. He tried poetry. He was terrible at it.

Madrid bombed by the fascists

GUERNICA AND THE
SECOND WORLD WAR

One evening in 1936, at his regular haunt, a café called 'Les Deux Magots', Picasso saw a woman take off her elegant gloves and begin to stab a dagger between her spreadeagled fingers. She frequently missed, and the tablecloth was spattered with blood. This, he thought, was the woman for him. Dora Maar was the most intelligent female that Picasso had ever met, a strikingly good-looking photographer and painter who lived with her parents. Picasso did not actually give up Marie-Thérèse and, tragically for both women – and Picasso's ego – they simply appear to have accepted his blatant infidelity. He was once quoted as saying that he looked upon very few women as truly human. Dora, however, at least had a trade, in his eyes. She was just beginning to teach him how to develop photos on his own when, in July 1936, news came through of the outbreak of the Spanish Civil War. Picasso declared for the Republic and the Spanish government appointed him director of the Prado Musem. The title was purely honorific, but it mattered a good deal to Picasso, who wanted to do his bit for Spain.

On 26 April, the Basque town of Guernica was bombed and destroyed by Nazi aircraft supporting Franco's forces. Civilian casualties, then relatively unknown in warfare, were horrific. 'In the picture I'm now painting – and which I shall call *Guernica* – and in all my recent work, I am expressing my horror of the military caste which is now plunging Spain into an ocean of misery and death,' wrote Picasso in May. The canvas, probably his best-known work, is immense – 20 feet across and 12 feet high. There is a total lack of colour – representing the stunned silence of a world after destruction. An electric light bulb hangs, still burning in the middle of the frame above a shrieking horse. A horrified woman leans in through a window in despair, while another figure lies mangled and trapped in disjointed wreckage. To one side, a mother cradles her dead baby, yelling in grief. It is a huge work which mixes neo-classical, Cubist and pastoral influences and, from the moment it was exhibited, it excited admiration,

Portrait of Dora Maar, 1937 by Picasso

astonishment and controversy. Whatever one thinks of *Guernica* artistically, it was a landmark painting historically.

Picasso was now fifty-seven and it was 1938. The Second World War was imminent and the Spanish Civil War was drawing to a miserable end. In December Picasso set up two centres for starving children, one in Barcelona and one in Madrid, donating two hundred thousand francs to each. Then, on 13 January 1939, his mother, Doña María, died. His grief was compounded when, on 26 January, his beloved Barcelona fell to Franco's fascists. That same year he was to have twelve exhibitions running simultaneously in the US until, in September, as he continued work on Dora Maar, war was declared in Europe.

In May 1940, German forces invaded

Guernica, 1935 by Picasso

Holland and Belgium and, after some seven weeks of blitzkrieg, utterly defeated the forces, mainly French and British, that had faced them. France surrendered on 22 June, and Paris, as well as roughly half of the rest of the country, was occupied by the Nazis.

Picasso was in a particularly precarious position, being a foreigner with known Communist links, but still he stayed in Paris. He lived in Saint-Germain and, though the majority of his friends had fled, he had Dora Maar to play with as well as Marie-Thérèse and Maïa. In 1941 he wrote a play called *Desire Caught by the Tail*, described as 'a cruel farce . . . based on the obsessions of cold, hunger, and love'. Early in 1944, friends organised a reading in which parts were taken by, among others, Jean-Paul Sartre, Simone de Beauvoir, and Raymond Queneau, under the direction of Albert Camus. Even the presence of such leading intellectual lights is unlikely to have done much for the quality of the play, however. Meanwhile, he painted in sombre, muted colours, with, given increasingly stringent rationing, an unsurprising emphasis on food. During the summer of 1942, deportations began and Picasso sculpted a seminal work from scrap metal called *Man with sheep*. It was 7 feet high and stood in his studio, becoming something of a symbolic beacon for the oppressed Parisians of the period. He himself rarely went out, but in 1943, on one of his very rare excursions, he met Françoise Gilot, a twenty-one-year-old then studying law at the Sorbonne. Picasso was immediately taken with her – she was young, red-haired, and somewhat aristocratic – and offered, quite literally, to show her his etchings. In June

Françoise Gillot

1944, the Allies landed in Normandy, and on 23 August Paris was liberated. France was free once more.

AFTER THE WAR

That Picasso had survived the Occupation was headline news; his decision, in 1945, to declare himself a Communist (he had joined the Party just after the liberation), made front pages around the world. He had metamorphosed from being a well-known painter to being an almost holy icon, constantly surrounded by admirers and hangers-on.

One of these, Geneviève Laporte, had turned up, aged seventeen, at his door in 1944 and asked to interview him about Marxism for her school magazine. It appeared that Picasso had never read anything either by or about Karl Marx, but he was charmed by her graceful youth and she began to visit him regularly. Eventually, this was to become a full-blown affair. His relationship with Françoise Gilot deteriorated, and he would turn on her constantly for no apparent reason. By 1945 Françoise saw less of him while Dora Maar still waited in her flat around the corner, permanently at his beck and call. As soon as he summoned her Dora would leap to be by his side, though, once there she would remain mute and unhappy. On one occasion she arrived for dinner stunningly late and then immediately left again. Picasso hurried after her, and brought her back, only to discover that she was suffering from hallucinations, and was obviously about to suffer a nervous breakdown. She screamed at him, 'As an artist you may be extraordinary, but morally speaking you're worthless.' Then Paul Éluard, the poet, who happened to be at the dinner, agreed with Dora, thumping a chair on the floor so passionately that it smashed into small pieces. Picasso was puzzled. He attributed Dora's behaviour to her following of the Surrealist movement, which advocated irrationality, while he found Éluard's attitude incomprehensible.

By the summer of 1945, Parisians began to return to the city from forced-labour or concentration camps in Germany and elsewhere, many looking like walking skeletons. Picasso now began work on his final really major work – *The Charnel House* – a large canvas all in black, grey and white with some still-life objects at top left and a tumbled heap of bodies, lifeless and silent, in contrast to the most striking figures in *Guernica*, in the foreground. It is a Cubist painting, but one with a direct message, though the message seems somewhat forced. Faced with such direct human suffering as the Holocaust, Picasso was at a loss.

In late summer, civilians were allowed petrol once more and Picasso took Dora Maar, who was still ill, to the south of France, where he bought her a house; he also paid for Geneviève to go to college in the United States. Now only Françoise, of all his women, was left in Paris, and he therefore asked her to live with him. In the spring of 1946 he began a kind of portrait of her, known as *Woman-Flower*, in which her body is the stem of a flower and her hair is made up of leaves. Later he made an engraving entitled *The Rape of*

In Sheffield, 1950

Europa, depicting Françoise astride a virile bull. Not long afterwards, in May 1947, she gave birth to a son whom they named Claude.

They went to live in the South of France where, bizarrely, they were continually pestered and followed by Olga Picasso who had suddenly appeared in the neighbourhood. Picasso merely shrugged, and took up working with ceramics, Vallauris, near where he lived, being a centre for the potter's art. He made hundreds of pots, decorated in an ancient Greek style, and, all the while, Olga constantly turned up at the house, often trying to hit Françoise. Picasso locked himself in his studio and ignored both women.

In August 1948, with Françoise once again pregnant, the Communist Party of Russia organised a 'Congress of Intellectuals for Peace' in Poland, and they invited Picasso to attend. Taking Paul Éluard with him, he flew in an aeroplane for the first time in his life. Otherwise, however, it was an extremely boring event and on his return, despite having brought with him gifts from Warsaw, Françoise greeted Picasso with a punch in the face, then locked herself in her son's bedroom. A little later, in January 1949, Picasso was asked to provide a poster for another Communist event, the Peace Congress, which was to be held in Paris. Since he didn't bother to do so, one of the organisers went to Picasso's unoccupied studio in Paris and picked out a lithograph which was lying around. This was the white dove which appeared overnight on hoardings all over Paris. As a symbol, it proved to be hugely successful, and Picasso was terribly

Paloma

pleased. Then, on 19 April, during the Peace Congress, Françoise gave birth, and he named his brand-new baby daughter Paloma, the Spanish word for dove.

In Provence, he began using the local rubbish heap as a source of materials for sculpture, and it was around this time that he made *The She-goat*, one of his best-known pieces, which dates from March 1950. Once again Picasso had grown bored with family life, however, and he began another affair with Geneviève Laporte, who had returned to France in 1950, having now become a poet. Picasso admired her work, and, particularly, her discretion. He also went to Sheffield to attend yet another peace conference, where he found he was the only foreign artist who had not been turned back at Dover. Picasso was furious to learn that he was considered to be so benign. Paulo,

Picasso and Clouzot

his son by Olga, became his permanent chauffeur, and the two of them returned to the South of France (from Paris) for his seventieth birthday in 1951. Meanwhile, Picasso was becoming increasingly involved with Geneviève, and increasingly estranged from Françoise.

In August 1952 he began work to convert his local chapel in Vallauris into a temple of peace, something for which he had begun sketching in the spring of that year. He would get up late each day, start work at eleven or twelve, go for a swim at lunchtime, and then work for nine or ten hours at a stretch. By October it was installed but the first two panels of *War and Peace* were a critical failure, and Picasso therefore never continued with the third. Then, in November, he heard that Paul Éluard, his closest friend, had died in

Paris, and Françoise, now almost certain that there was another woman on the scene, threatened to leave. Geneviève retreated to the countryside. For Picasso, there were other sadnesses, too: Matisse was very ill; Braque no longer spoke to him. Picasso, who hated the thought of being alone, begged Françoise to stay. She was not at all keen, but help was at hand. Jacqueline Hutin, *née* Roque, who had recently divorced her husband, an engineer, now lived nearby with her daughter, Kathy. She was tiny and neat, twenty-seven years old and almost wholly uneducated. Picasso was by now an old man, though neither his looks nor his demeanour betrayed this, and he wanted someone to be young with. Jacqueline was thrilled to accompany him on many extravagant displays of sociability – gambling in nightclubs, dancing at Saint-Tropez, dining out (with Picasso once

Claude, Paloma and Paul, 1966

wearing a red nose and a false moustache). On 30 September 1953, Françoise told him that she was leaving for good, and that she was taking the children with her. That day she, Claude and Paloma returned to Paris.

Picasso, who wasn't totally satisfied with Jacqueline, returned to Paris and asked Geneviève to live with him. They had not seen each other for over a year and she demurred for ten minutes. This was too slow for Picasso. He drove home alone. Back in the south, beween 1953 and 1954, he produced a collection of over 180 drawings, known as the *Verve Suite,* which displayed an obsessive interest in the female body. He also began several portraits of Jacqueline Hutin, though he told his friends that he could not possibly go to bed with a woman who had had a child by another man. Françoise returned with the children and Picasso begged her to stay but she rejected him. Picasso begged his older daughter, Maïa, to come from Paris and to sleep in a spare bed in his room, which she did. He could not bear to spend the whole night entirely alone.

In 1955 Jacqueline Hutin turned up again. Maïa had to return to Paris and Jacqueline simply moved into her empty bed. During the next few weeks Picasso was astonishingly rude to her in company, whilst she spoke to him in the third person, referred to him as her god, and frequently kissed his hands. To general astonishment, Picasso took her home to Vallauris where he began painting her as a plump, comfortable little figure. Françoise, meanwhile, announced that she planned to marry a man called Simon; she and Picasso were never to see each other again. Money

At work (from *The Picasso Mystery*)

was, in the meantime, rolling in – Picasso was now the richest painter ever to have lived.

That year, 1955, also brought a Picasso retrospective at the Louvre, as well as the first documentary about him – *The Picasso Mystery*, directed by Georges Clouzot. Picasso was seized with enthusiasm for the medium and painted on transparent glass so that the camera could film him through this transparent 'canvas' as he worked. He was increasingly surrounded by idolising admirers whom he referred to as 'the courtiers', and money no longer had any meaning for him. When, in 1958, he was told that a seventeenth-century castle, the Château de Vauvenargues, near Arles, was for sale, Picasso bought it within forty-eight hours, only having seen it once.

Picasso at the Galerie Matarasso, Nice, 1956

In the château he hung his collection of paintings which, besides his own pieces, now included works by Matisse, Braque, Cézanne, Degas, Rousseau, and Renoir, and he painted Jacqueline as the queen of the mansion. In 1960, 450,000 people saw the London retrospective of his work at the Tate Gallery. Meanwhile, fans, celebrity hunters, and the plain curious arrived in droves at Vauvenargues, peering through the gates with binoculars. Picasso could no longer bear it, and, in 1961, he moved out again, this time to Notre-Dame-de-Vie, a country house near Mougins, also in Provence. On 2 March that same year he married Jacqueline in extreme secrecy, with only two witnesses present. He was almost eighty, and she thirty-five. She stood to gain millions by the ceremony and, eventually, she did.

Picasso and Jacqueline, 1961

In 1963 the Picasso Museum in Barcelona finally opened. Then, in 1964, Françoise Gilot brought out a book, *Life With Picasso*, which portrayed the artist as an evil, manipulative and selfish man. The book attracted worldwide media interest and became a major bestseller, and his hatred of Françoise redoubled. Though his son and daughter by Françoise, Claude and Paloma, knew nothing of the row, they were never to see him again. Each time they arrived at Notre-Dame-de-Vie, they were turned away, as were Maïa, his eldest daughter, and Pablito and Marina, his son Paulo's children. Picasso's children and grandchildren blamed this rejection on the malevolent influence of his new wife, but it seems unlikely that such a timid woman could have had such a powerful effect on her god, even in his eighties.

Picasso

The god himself carried on drawing and Picasso came as close as he ever got to writing a will – prompted by General Franco, who begged him to let *Guernica* come to Spain. A specially completed room at the Museum of Modern Art in Madrid had been built for the painting, and Picasso stipulated in writing that it should go to Spain but only 'when the Republican liberties are restored'. In the meantime, he gave fifty drawings to a museum in Arles and the cubist *Guitar* of 1912–13 to the Museum of Modern Art in New York. His failure to make a formal disposal of most of his other goods, now worth millions, was to mean years of ugly, legal wrangling among family and friends after his death.

In 1971 he was ninety. There were worldwide celebrations to mark his birthday, and the great gallery in the Louvre was rehung to accommodate eight of his works – something which had never before happened to a living artist. Picasso didn't attend the opening. Over the next few years he completed hundreds of drawings of Jacqueline, the Musée Picasso opened in Paris, and he continued to produce ceramics. But his paintings had now become harsh and brutal, often representing whores with their legs spread wide, depicted in cold black and white. Pablito, wanting to see his grandfather, climbed the walls of the house, only to be set upon by guard dogs and taken away by the police. Picasso became known as the hermit of Mougins, and on 8 April 1973, he died with Jacqueline by his side. She had him buried at the chateau he had come to detest – Vauvenargues.